I0173171

Hey Bestie

"Poems for the Friends Who Still Feels Like Home"

Pooja

/ BookLeaf
Publishing

India | USA | UK

Made with ❤ on the BookLeaf Publishing Platform
www.bookleafpub.in
www.bookleafpub.com

Dedication

To Dost—my muse, my anchor, my home.
And to my family—especially my mother,
(つ´▽｀)つ

This book holds little pieces of us:
our hugs, our smiles, our quiet strength.
It's not just my story—it's ours.
Thank you for standing by me when I felt unsure,
for believing in me when things were hard,
and for always being there with kindness and care.
"You helped me be brave and true,
and I'll carry that with me always."

Preface

This book began with a teddy—one that shares your name. Every time I see it, I'm reminded of us. Of the movie nights that turned into therapy sessions, the chicken cravings that led to spontaneous food hunts, and the online shopping sprees that felt like healing. We were inseparable once. Life moves differently now, and we've both grown in our own ways. But even in the quiet, you're still my favorite notification. *(✿˘⌣˘✿)*

You're the heart of this book. My muse. The reason these poems exist. Around you, there was always a constellation of calm—friends who showed up in tea breaks, in festival plans, in emojis, in voice notes, and in those perfectly timed "you okay?" check-ins. This book is my way of saying: I miss you. I appreciate you. And I'll always choose this friendship, even if it whispers from a distance. Some friendships don't need daily conversations to stay alive—they live quietly in memories, in feelings, in the little things.

Acknowledgements

To all my friends—those who stayed, and those who drifted—thank you.

You've been my chaos coordinators, snack critics, late-night therapists, and accidental life coaches.

Some are still here, cheering me on. Some left quietly, but not without leaving a lesson.

I needed both. Every friendship helped me grow, spiral, laugh—and write this book. So this is for you too.

To the Bestie who inspired every line—

Thank you for being my favorite notification, my chicken partner, and the reason my cart is never empty.

You've shown up in silence and celebration, in festivals and those rare catch-up calls that feel like no time has passed.

To BookLeaf Publishing—

Thank you for turning memory into poetry and chaos into comfort.

Your 21-Day Challenge didn't just publish my words—it helped me find the people behind them.

(ᵔ◡ᵔ)/

To every reader who's ever missed a friend—this book is for you.

Day 1. My Everyday

Hey Bestie,
You were my "good morning" glow,
Before the world began to overflow.
My comfort line before the meal,
You made the ordinary feel surreal.
(✿˘︶˘✿)
No plans, no fuss, just you and me—
A screen, some tea, and quiet glee.
Even tired, you'd still appear,
Ask about my day, stay near.
(づ｡◕‿‿◕｡)づ
We had a rhythm, soft and true,
Not perfect—just me and you.
Now life scrolls in endless streams,
But I still drift to quiet dreams.
Of carts we filled but left behind,
Of love that never changed with time.
And though we don't talk every day,
A part of me still wants to stay.
(o´∧`o)('•ᴗ•`)
"Teri kami mein chai bhi feeki lagti hai."
(Without you, even tea tastes bland.)

1

Day 2 . Movie Buddy

Hey Bestie,
You never teased,
Not when my theories were unleashed.
Paused the scene, rewound with flair—
"You see? The villain's right there!"
(Ο_Ο)
You loved action, bold and loud,
Heroes walking through fire, proud.
I cried at portals, speeches too,
While you just munched and nodded through.
(¬_¬)
I talked through credits, trailers, plot,
You let me—never said "stop."
No fancy plans, just screen and snack,
My voice filling every crack.
(ˆ‿ˆ)ﾉ
Now when I press play alone,
I still talk, like you're on the phone.
Still feel you smiling, calm and true—
Because that's just us: me and you.
(o˙∧˙o)″(≧‿≦)
Tere bina scene chalu hai... par maza nahi aa raha.
 (The scene's still playing... but it's just not fun without you.)

Day 3. Meltdown Buddy

Hey Bestie,
I showed up with a syllabus and a meltdown.
You showed up with chicken.
Guess who saved the day?
(＾⌣＾)

I ranted about exams like they were boss fights.
You listened like it was a podcast—
no judgment, just bites and nods.
(¬‿¬)

You never said, "Calm down."
You just passed the ketchup
and let me spiral in peace.
(¬‿¬)

I'd say things like,
"I might fall flat,"
"I'm changing paths—imagine that!"
"Do clouds know where they're meant to be?"
"Is drifting just a way to see?"
(¬‿¬)

You didn't flinch.
You just ordered more.
We didn't solve anything,
but somehow,
after food and friendship,
everything felt less scary.
(づ｡◦＿＿◦｡)づ

Even now, when I panic alone,
I think of you—
the calm in my chaos,
the chicken in my crisis,
the friend who never needed to fix me
to make me feel okay.

(´ ˘ `)♡
Tumhare saath life thodi kam stressful lagti hai
(With you, life feels a little less stressful.)

4

Day 4. Shopping Buddy

Hey Bestie,
We've walked the streets,
from window shops to online treats.
You knew the tricks, the hidden hacks,
the perfect gift, the best-priced snacks.
(ʕ•ﻌ•ʔ)

We'd wander lanes with zero plan,
then spot a steal and say, "I ran!"
You'd bargain like a seasoned pro,
while I just smiled and let it flow.
(¬_¬)

Online, we'd send each other links—
gadgets, hoodies, skincare things.
"Buy me this," "I'll gift you that,"
our chats were basically retail chat.
(≧◡≦)

You knew the deals in every zone—
tech, fashion, food, unknown.
I'd rant about prices, sigh and scroll,
you'd find the coupon, play your role.
(✿˘︶˘✿)

Even now, when I shop alone,
I hear your voice on speakerphone.
"Don't buy that," "Wait for the sale,"
"Add to cart, but don't derail."
(づ｡◕‿‿◕｡)づ

You weren't my crush or secret muse—
you were the friend I'd never lose.
My wish list buddy, my retail thrill,
the one who made my cart feel full.

———————————————————————

(^ᴗ^)
Tu ho toh discount bhi dosti lagti hai
(With you, even discounts feel like friendship.)

Day 5. Listener Buddy

Hey Bestie,

We didn't meet in class or hall—
 we met mid-chaos, after it all.
 And somehow, through every twist and turn,
 you became the calm I didn't earn.
(✿˘︶˘✿)

I'd spiral, rage, overshare with flair,
you'd sit in silence, always there.
Like my drama was a podcast stream,
and you were tuned in—no need to scream.
(¬‿¬)

You knew my cast: the queen, the mess,
the ones who caused emotional stress.
I'd say, "Don't judge me, I'm a storm,"
you'd say, "I'm used to your weather norm."
(◉‿◉)

Screenshots turned into quiet proof,
voice notes met your silent truth.
And every gossip, wild or deep,
felt like a hug that let me sleep.
(づ｡◦＿＿◦｡)づ

You didn't fix me, didn't preach,
just stayed within my storm's reach.
And somehow, in your gentle way,
you made my anger drift away.

(ꑄˇ‿ˇꑄ)
Tum ho toh dil gaata hai
Tum na ho toh sab kuch khamosh lagta hai.
(When you're here, my heart sings—
 when you're not, everything feels silent.)

Day 6. Travel Buddy

Hey Bestie,
We didn't chase the travel thrill,
just car rides, laughs, and one short chill.
That wedding? We dressed up right,
clicked some pics, danced through the night.
(≧∪≦)

Snowy day, no grand parade,
just cold air and jokes we made.
You took my photos, caught the glow,
while I posed awkward in the snow.
(∩‿∩)

House parties, rooftops, fairy lights,
music, snacks, and cozy nights.
From birthdays to random scenes,
we turned rooftops into party dreams.
(ﾉ‿ﾉ)ﾉ🎉

Cafes, parks, and food court stops,
felt like travel without the hops.
No big plans, no fancy roam—
just friends who made each place feel home.
(づ｡◕‿‿◕｡)づ

But that boat ride? My favorite part—
drizzle, tea, and a full-heart start.
We laughed by the ghat, made dreamy plans,
still waiting to happen, like untouched sands.
(✿˘︶˘✿)

We planned big—Goa, hills, food spree,
but even missed trips felt carefree.
Because with you, it's crystal clear—
every small moment felt sincere.

(ღ˘︶˘ღ)
Tum ho toh har mod par manzil milti hai
(With you, every turn feels like a destination.)

Day 7. Teddy and You

Hey Bestie,

I had the teddy way before you came,
but guess what? It shares your name.
Coincidence? Destiny? Plot twist divine?
Either way, the timing was fine.
(O_O)

It's soft, it's quiet, it never complains—
basically you, minus the brain.
It's seen my snack attacks at 2 AM,
and survived my "I'm done with him!" mayhem.
(π∼π)

When you annoy me (which you do, FYI),
the teddy gets a punch—not gonna lie.
No hard feelings, just plushy pain,
he bounces back. You'd do the same.
(つ˘_˘)つ

It listens to rants, sits through my mess,
and never judges my outfit stress.
Not a cuddlemate, don't get weird—
just a fluffball that's always cheered.
(ʕ•ɞ•ʔ)

So no, I didn't name it for you,
but now it feels like déjà vu.
Same name, same vibe, same silent stare—
like you're sneakily always there.

_____

(ˆ‿ˆ)
Naam pehle se tha, par attitude bhi match karta hai.
(The name came first—but the attitude? That's a perfect match.)

Day 8. Pooh Square

Hey Pooh,

You walked into my gym routine
and turned it into a daily scene.
Not just squats and protein shakes,
but tea-time talks and study breaks.
(≧‿≦)

You glow when goals are on your mind,
with dreams so big, yet heart so kind.
You cook with love (and spice galore),
even if toast ends up on the floor.
(ᄀ‿ᄀ)

You dragged me to the doc one day,
like "No excuses, come what may!"
Then fed me food that healed my soul,
and made me laugh till I lost control.
(₀♥‿♥₀)

We don't meet daily, that's okay,
but when we do—it's tiffin day!
Packed with gossip, hugs, and cheer,
and "you've got this" in your gear.
(づ ̄ ³ ̄)づ

Nine years strong, and still the same—
same vibe, same soul, same name.
I cry at ads, you quote the wise,
but together? We're Poohs who rise.
(✿ᴖ‿ᴖ)

And in this gym-life epic tale,
Bahubali shows up without fail—
like a flex cameo, blink and he's gone,
but the vibe he leaves? Full-on!
(·ᗢ·)ʒ
        (ง •̀_•́)ง
              (つ´ヮ`)つ

There was so much noise, people so fast,
but our teatime made the joy last.
Bahubali smiled, calm and kind,
we shared our stories, left worries behind.
No fancy things, no big loud cheer,
just warm tea and friends so dear.
(ˆ‿ˆ)つ

In a world that moves so fast and loud,
our friendship feels like a soft, safe cloud.
No need for noise, no need to try—
just quiet care that lifts us high.
*(˘︶˘).｡.:♡

We don't talk much, and that's okay,
because bond like ours doesn't fade away.
A reel, a smile, a memory shared—
proof that we've always truly cared.
(´₀•˘•₀`)

So, here's to us, calm and true,
to Pooh, Bahubali, and me with you.
This bond we have—it's deep, it's wide,
a peaceful place where hearts reside.

• (づ｡◦ ◦｡)づ

Naam ek, vibe same—Bahubali bhi sath.

(Same name, same vibe—Bahubali's with us too.)

Day 9. ParleG

Dear ParleG,

You never preached or made a fuss,

You simply showed up—just like us.

At the gym, with motivation and plan,

On Sundays too, you always ran.

(•ᴗ•)ﻭ

You helped me lift—not just the weight,

But heavy thoughts I couldn't state.

Lazy days and restless minds,

You healed me in your silent kinds.

(˘ᴗ˘)

We didn't talk of pain or fear,

We laughed, we trained, you stayed sincere.

No deep confessions, no loud display,

Just "Chai?"—and the gloom would drift away.

(˘ᴗ˘♡)

Your name? A tribute, sweet and true—
To Parle-G biscuits you once loved too.
Chai and those snacks, your perfect pair,
Till people said, "Don't eat that there."
You gave them up, though they brought you joy,
Like a kid parting with his favorite toy.
But I still smile when I hear your name,
Because Parleg, you're still the same.
(๑ ˃ᴗ˂)

You taught me strength is calm and clear,
It's showing up, just being near.
It's being there, no need to try,
Just one warm sip and a knowing eye.
(✿╭╮)

Thanks for being my steady light,
My post-gym calm, my Sunday might.
A friend who didn't need to shout,
But knew what showing up's about.

(づ｡◕‿‿◕｡)づ
"Dosti har baar shabd nahi maangti,
Kabhi ek cup chai bhi kaafi hoti hai."
(Friendship doesn't always need words—
Sometimes, a cup of chai is more than enough.)

Day 10. Spiritual Guide

Hey Soul,

We met in pixels, not in place,
Yet your words held a quiet grace.
Like stars that glow but never shout,
You lit the path when I had doubt.
(o •́ _•̀o)

You spoke of crystals, books, and light,
Of energy that feels just right.
Of patience born from deep inside,
Not waiting—but a trustful stride.
(˘ ˘ "♡)

You saw my soul before I could,
And told me magic's in my blood.
Not just kind or smart or wise—
But stardust wrapped in human guise.
(o •́ _•̀o)

When I spiraled, lost in fear,
You didn’t fix, you stayed near.
“Feel it. You’re allowed,” you said,
And peace bloomed where panic spread.
(´｡• ᵕ •｡`)

You always said I’m perfect still,
Adored me deeply and always will.
“You’re gifted, bright, a voice so clear—
Why hide your light or doubt your cheer?”
(๑•́ ₃ •̀๑)

You asked me why I shrink my flame,
Why I forget my own sweet name.
“You’re meant to fly, not fear the sky—
So, chase your joy, don’t question why.”
(•̀ᴗ•́)و

I’ve made delays, I’ve lost some time,
But you remind me I still can climb.
You promised me you’d always stay,
To guard my heart and light the way.
(づ￣ ³￣)づ

Even now, when I forget my worth,
You remind me of my magic birth.
A soul, a spark, a voice so true—
And say, "I'm proud to walk with you."
(✿⌒‿⌒)

I'll wear my light, a crown so bright,
 Embracing both the dark and light.
 For in this dance of joy and ache,
 I find the strength I used to chase.
(₀˙ᵕ-)✧ (⌒‿⌒)*

With every breath, I rise again,
A phoenix born from past and pain.
Through trials met and shadows faced,
Your love remains—a gentle grace.

(₀˙⌒˙₀)人(₀˙‿˙₀)
"Jo roshni andar se aati hai,
 Wahi andheron ko mitaati hai."
The light that rises from within
 Is the one that makes darkness thin.

Day 11. Big Reaper

Hey Reaper,
You left the game, but not the thread—
Your loyalty lingered, softly spread.
No final quest, no loud goodbye,
Just orbiting calm beneath my sky.
(｡•́‿•̀｡)

We met in pixels, side by side,
Shared raids, late chats, and quiet pride.
Then life called louder than the screen,
And you chose roots, not just routine.
(˘͈ ᵕ ˘͈♡)

You paint in strokes that speak in hush—
Abstract, deep, a mindful rush.
Each canvas holds what words can't say,
A soul in bloom, a quiet way.
(｡•́‿•̀｡)

Your daughter asked, "Why stare so long?"
And you recalled where hearts belong.
Now coffee brews and gardens grow,
Where once your avatar would glow.
(´ₒ• ˇ •ₒ`)

You're a protector, through and through—
A soldier's heart, both fierce and true.
You traded guns for brush and soil,
But still defend with quiet toil.
(づ ̄ ³ ̄)づ

The parrots perch, the snakes stay near,
Even wild things feel safe right here.
Your cats curl close, your dogs adore—
You're nature's friend, and so much more.
(✿⌒‿⌒)

You carry years like steady flame,
Not loud, not proud—just not the same.
With every word, you guide with grace,
A friend whose calm still holds its place.
(ₒ˙ᵕ-)✧

You said I brought you peace at last,
A quiet balm for battles past.
And I replied, with heart laid bare—
No matter what, I'm always there.
(o ˙‿˙o)

Now seasons shift and stories fade,
But some connections never trade.
You may be offline, out of sight,
Yet in my world, you're still a light.

(o ♥‿♥o)
"Sipahi se kalākār ban gaye ho,
 Aur kuch dosti logout ke baad bhi jeeti rehti ho."
("From soldier to artist, you changed your way,
 And some friendships still choose to stay.")

Day 12. My crew

Hey furries,
Siquis, Senze, Indigo, MehLa,
Michael, Lilmissy—my Honey gala.
You weren't just names on a glowing screen,
You were my crew, my in-between.
(o•́‿•̀o)

You cheered my chaos, sparked my flair,
Knew when I needed love or air.
No maps, no meetups, yet somehow knew
When I was low, or bursting through.
(̆ ᵕ ̆♡)

You let me be loud, you let me be strange,
You danced with my dreams, no need to change.
We built a den from pixel dust,
With puns and plans and mutual trust.
(o•́‿•̀o)

Late-night chats and inside jokes,
Ideas that bloomed like fire and oaks.
You made the game feel soft and wide,
A hug that loaded from inside.
(´o•ᵕ•o`)

In State 143, I found two more—
Shadow and Steel knight, hearts I adore.
They joined the map, they lit the way,
Two stars that brighten every day.
(づ ̄ ³ ̄)づ
Now it feels like Michael, and I are left at home,
while the rest of the family has scattered—
not just changed but moved to different states.
It's strange. It's quiet. It's life.
(O_O)
I promise to meet you on attack days,
on my Saturdays, shield on—just to say hi.
Maybe I'll join your state.
Maybe you'll move back.
Who knows?
That's the thing about life—it scrolls forward,
but some tabs stay open.
(｡•ᴗ-)✧
And then came Hopeville, State 54,
Where Mama Bear leads with love and lore.
We're cubs beneath her steady gaze,
A team that lifts in quiet ways.
BigReaper, Mystiq, Drwub, conk,
Badone, Chimlin, Thunderbeast,—our pride,
Forever missed, still by our side.
(✿∩_∩)

Hopeville came with Mama Bear's care,
She leads with kindness, always fair.
We're still a family, strong and wide,
With love and laughter on every side.
Hannibal, Mmaori, Elsnakeeye, Josharoo,
Ashley, Blueblood, Sonis, Rudefoot too,
Ahsan Dhar, Cdawg, Sil, Villain in view—
Each one shines in their own way,
In my heart, they'll always stay.
(✿◠‿◠) (o˙ᴗ-)✧
Two homes, two screens, one soul that roams—
Yet every chat still feels like home.
You proved that bonds don't need a street—
Just hearts that sync and pixels that meet.
Even when states and teams may shift,
The love we built is still a gift.

(o♥‿♥o)

"Na jagah thi, na zarurat thi raah—Bas tum the, aur dosti ka narm sa gahraah."

("No place, no path, no need to roam— Just you, and friendship, feeling like home.")

Day 13 . Soulspice

You speak like a recipe, warm and wise–
With layers of truth and no disguise.
A pinch of passion, a simmered thought,
You stir the feelings most forget or fought.
(｡•́‿•̀｡)

You treat food like a sacred tongue,
Where every flavor's gently sung.
And somehow, even through the screen,
You made my silence feel seen.
(˘͈ ᵕ ˘͈♡)

You explain too much, and I adore
The way you open every door.
Each thought unpacked, each feeling named–
A spice of care, never ashamed.
(*ꈍᴗꈍ*)

You're emotional, but never weak—
You feel with depth, you boldly speak.
You show me how soft hearts can fight,
And how quiet souls still shine bright.
(´₀• ˘ •₀`)
You're still exploring what you're here to do,
But I already see the truth in you—
In how you love, in how you try,
In how you lift without asking why.
(づ￣ ³￣)づ
You care for animals, listen deep,
You carry promises others don't keep.
Even tired, you still appear—
A peaceful soul who stays sincere.
(✿⌒‿⌒)
And when I talk too much, too fast,
You catch the parts that others pass.
You hear the ache behind the cheer,
You make the noise feel less unclear.
(₀˙ᵕ-)✧

(₀♥‿♥₀)
"Main bolti hoon, par sunta kaun?
Phir tum aaye—jaise ek sukoon ka gaon."
(I speak and speak, but who can hear?
Then you arrived—and brought me near.)

Day 14. Metro moon

Hey Moon,
We don’t talk much or share too deep,
But still your calm helps mine to keep.
You show up soft, without a fuss,
Like evening light that rides with us.
(｡•́‿•̀｡)

We meet, we eat, we share a seat,
No words exchanged, but still it’s sweet.
The silence sits between each bite,
And somehow, everything feels right.
(˘͈ ᵕ ˘͈♡)

You ask me gently, “Are you okay?”
Not in a loud or showy way.
Just like a breeze that passes through,
It’s quiet, kind, and feels like you.
(*꒦ິ꒳꒦ີ*)

You help me move without a sound,
No big advice, no crowd around.
You show me healing doesn’t need
A stage, a light, or someone’s lead.
(´｡• ᵕ •｡`)

Thanks for being my silent cheer,
My food-time friend who feels sincere.
Not close enough for hugs or calls,
But still you catch me when life stalls.
The one who says "Koi Na" slow—
And somehow helps the worry go.
(o˙ᵕ-)✧

I'm glad we met. Though not too near,
Your quiet grace still feels sincere.
You've made my world, in your own way,
A softer place on busy days.

(o♥_♥o)
"Bina shabdon ke jo saath ho,
Wahi toh asli raahat ho."
("The one who stays without a sound,
Is often where true peace is found.")

30

15. Chordmate

Hey Chordie,

You didn't just teach me how to play—
You taught me how to feel the day.
To pause between the highs and lows,
To let joy linger as it flows.
(｡•́‿•̀｡)

Your voice? A tune that softly stays,
Not just in ears, but in my days.
Like when you cheered my job success,
With laughter, chords, and party mess.
(˘̩̩ᵕ˘̩̩♡)

We didn't jam each afternoon,
But when we did, it felt like June.
The world tuned in, the vibe was right—
Our friendship sang in shared delight.
(｡•́‿•̀｡)

You made each strum a celebration,
Not bound by rules or expectation.
You showed me music's sweetest part—
Is playing from a present heart.
(´｡• ᵕ •｡`)

Thanks for being my rhythm guide,
My party spark, my joyful tide.
The melody that helped me see
That milestones hum in harmony.
(o˙ᴗ-)✦

I'm glad we met.
Your joy, your tone—
Still echo when I'm on my own.

(o♥‿♥o)
**"Har khushi mein jo sur mil jaaye,
Wahi toh dosti ka geet ban jaaye."**
*("When joy and rhythm intertwine,
That's when friendship starts to shine.")*

Day 16. Devi Ma's Child,

Hey Tuntun,
We met in a season of strength and sweat,
Between gym sets and meals well set.
Your chicken was warm, your presence kind,
A quiet friend with a thoughtful mind.
(₀˙ᵕ-)✧

You lived with grace, with faith so deep,
Your goddess watched while the world would sleep.
The mantras hummed, the diya glowed,
And every plate with fragrance flowed.
(˘ᵕ˘♡)

You told me, "Don't wear blue today,"
"Wear red instead—it keeps harm away."
I smiled and said, "But red feels loud."
You frowned a bit, your voice was proud.
"Then who's yelling now?" I softly teased—
Blue is peace. It keeps me eased.
و(˙ᵕ˙)

We weren't too close, but we were kind,
A thread of care not tightly twined.
Then silence came, and you were gone,
No message left, no reason drawn.
(´｡• ᵕ •｡`)

I didn't call. You didn't too.
And maybe that was overdue.
But still I pray you're safe and free,
That life is kind, as it should be.
(｡♥‿♥｡)

Some ties don't knot, but still they stay—
In memory's quiet, gentle way.
You helped me heal, though we grew apart,
And left your warmth inside my heart.

_____

(｡•́‿•̀｡)つ
Jo dil se nikli baat rahi,
Wo tere naam ki prarthana rahi.
(*The words that left my heart unsaid,*
Still reach you as a prayer instead.)

Day 17. Ms Cutie

Hey Ms Cutie,
We strolled through streets with snacks in hand,
From pizza bites to golgappe stand.
You'd try it all, with sparkling eyes,
And rate each chai like it was a prize.
(｡•ᴗ-)✧

You'd shop with flair, in every lane,
Then cry, "I'm mota!"—here we go again.
We'd cheer you up, you'd strike a pose,
Stylo queen in thrifted clothes.
(•ᴗ•)و

You lit the mood, you made us laugh,
Even when life cut joy in half.
But slowly, time began to race,
And we both lost that meeting place.
(´｡• ᵕ •｡`)

I called, you were busy.
You called, I missed.
And now our bond
just feels like mist.
I wonder if your new crew stays,
Or if you miss our old-school days.
I miss our chai, our shopping spree,
The way you'd snack so joyfully.
But more than food, I miss your heart—
The one that healed with every start.
(ˇᵕ ˇ♡)

I pray you're happy,
snacking still,
With friends who love you
loud and chill.
May your future bloom,
your laughter stay—
And may our bond
return someday.

(ˇᵕ ˇ♡)つ
Jo saath chale the chai ke sang,
 Wo yaad rahe har dil ke rang._
The ones who walked with chai in hand, Stay in every
heart, in every little memory.

18. Ms VibeCart

Hey Princess,
You're the queen of every deal,
From food to rides to doctor's seal.
"Why step out?" you always say—
"Just tap the app and save the day!"
You've got a knack for online flair,
From snacks to meds, it's all right there.
(o•ᴗ-)✧

We met in coaching, vibe was tight,
You made the dullest days feel light.
Now you're my hotline, snack and soul,
You hype me up when I lose control.
"You're made for more," you always say,
"Just breathe it out, you'll find your way."
(˘ᴗ˘♡)

You're introvert, but friends just stick—
Like Shin Chan jokes and memes that click.
We rarely call, but when we do,
It's hours of "same!" and "me too, boo!"
You spill your tea, I spill mine too,
And somehow, life feels less askew.
(o•ᴗ-)✧

We watched his movie—pure delight,
A theatre trip that felt just right.
With Chinese platter, laughs so loud,
We made the staff feel extra proud.
You giggled hard, I spilled my tea,
Shin Chan would've blessed our spree.
(o•‿•o)

You love your dogs, your screen, your space,
You move through life with gentle grace.
No drama, guilt, or shady shade—
Just joy and jokes and memes well-made.
You're smart and cute, a vibe so rare,
With Shin Chan hair and Amazon flair.

(≧‿≦)つ✿
Shinchan jaisa jo hansi lutaaye,
Wo dost har din khaas banaaye.
The one who laughs like Shin Chan bright,
Makes every single day feel right.

Day 19. Ms SecretSpice

Hey Mishti,
We weren't in school for very long,
But still the bond felt deep and strong.
Then college came, and there you were—
Still cooking meals with chef-like flair.
Your hands knew spice, your heart knew taste,
No dish you made would go to waste.
(ₒ˙ᵕ-)✧
Your family shone with warmth and grace,
They welcomed me in every space.
At weddings, feasts, and festive nights,
We shared our laughs, our little bites.
Your brother cooked, you served with pride,
And I'd be there, right by your side.
(˘ᵥ ˘♡)

I paid the bills, the snacks, the show—
The movie nights, the street food glow.
I never asked for pay or praise,
Just friendship in its quiet phase.
But then you left, without a sound,
No invite came, no closure found.
(´ₒ• ˇ •ₒ`)

You chose to part, to keep it sealed,
But Tubelight knew—the truth revealed.
He got married too, but didn't drift,
He's still the bridge when bonds feel swift.
He meets me still, he stays around,
A friend who shows when I feel down.
(´o•ᵕ•o`)

And you? I wish you joy and light,
Though part of me still asks, "Was I right?"
Was I just there to pay, to serve?
Did I get less than I deserve?
But maybe not. Maybe that's fine.
Some ties don't last but still align.
(o•́‿•̀o)

I don't want meetings, don't want blame—
Just peace for you, and Tubelight's flame.
For all the food, the love, the grace,
I still remember every place.

(o•́ᴥ•̀o)⊃
Jo bina bataye door chali gayi,
Wo yaadein phir bhi paas rahi._
(The one who left without goodbye,
Still lives in memories that never die.)

20. Hey Crew

(˘ᵕ˘♡) (•̀ᴗ•́)و (´｡• ᵕ •｡)

Hey DBSH, you stayed so true—
Taught me when exams felt new.
Cute and funny, snack in hand,
You helped me learn, you helped me stand.
(｡•́‿•̀｡)

Hey Ms Banker, quiet, kind, and wise,
With steady grace and no disguise.
You flowed through life without a fuss,
But always made space just for us.
(˘ᵕ˘♡)

Hey Ms Judge, you spoke with silent care,
Your verdicts soft, your heart laid bare.
We met in college, calm and clear—
You ruled with warmth, not loud or fear.
(｡•́︿•̀｡)

Hey Professor A, my foodie friend,
Philosopher with thoughts that bend.
You gossip sweet, you eat with flair,
And teach with love, beyond compare.
(≧◡≦)

To those now married, **far away**,
Who helped me heal, then chose their way—
I thank you still, though names may fade,
Your kindness lives in how I've stayed.
(´｡• ᵕ •｡)
You showed up when I couldn't speak,
Held me strong when I felt weak.
No fanfare, just a gentle thread—
A "you'll be fine" when tears were shed.
(˘͈ᵕ˘͈♡)

I'm proud of you, each quiet soul,
You helped me stitch, you made me whole.
Even if we've lost the tune,
Your warmth still hums beneath my moon.

(*˘͈ᵕ˘͈*)
Jo chupchaap saath nibha gaye,
Woh sabse gehre nishaan chhod gaye.
The quiet ones who stayed, left the deepest marks.

21. My home

Hey Dost,

(ˇ̈ ˇ♡) (•◡•) و (o•́_•̀o)

I wrote a whole book just to say—
I missed you in that quiet way.
Not with drama, not with tears,
But in memes unsent for months and years.
In reels I saved but didn't share,
In jokes that hung mid-air.
(o•́ ∧ •̀o)

Life got loud, and I got swept—
Deadlines, calls, routines I kept.
We didn't fight, we didn't fall,
We just paused—like a missed call.
But even when the chats grew thin,
You stayed soft, like a hum within.
(ˇ̈ ˇ♡)

You were my calm, my true buddy,
My "try this sweet" and "watch part two."
You wrapped my birthdays in delight,
Remembered my quirks, got the playlist right.
Your gifts weren't grand, but they always fit—
A memory wrapped in perfect wit.

(≧◡≦)
We text in fragments, not full prose,
But every ping still gently shows
That even when the words are few,
You're still my mirror, still my glue.
You hugged me when I needed it—
No questions asked, no drama hit.
Just arms that knew, just eyes that saw—
You fixed me soft, without a flaw.
(´₀•ˇ•₀`)

You didn't ask why I went quiet,
You didn't start a friendship riot.
You just showed up, with food and grace,
And let me land in your safe space.
We talked of nothing, laughed till late—
And somehow that reset my fate.
(₀˙ᴗ-)✧

I saw you again—not just in view,
But in every memory stitched into you.
The festivals, the food, the fights,
The shoulder punch, the late-night bites.
(•ᴗ•)و (＊ˇ ˇ＊)

44

So here I am, the book complete—
Each page a pulse, each line a beat.
I named the stars, I stitched the sky,
But you're the thread I can't untie.
Not just a friend, not just a view—
"You are my home.
I circle back to you."
(ˇ˯ˇ♡) (づ｡◕‿‿◕｡)づ (｡♥‿♥｡)

No matter where the road may bend,
I want you near—my soul, my friend.
Even if "just friends" is where we land,
I'll hold your heart in open hand.
Our memories glow, they still shine through—
You're not just a friend... you're family too.

(ˇ˯ˇ♡) (o•‿•o)
"O nadan parinde, ghar aaja,
Tum bin ye ghar adhura hai."
("O naïve bird, come back home,
Without you, this house feels incomplete.")

www.ingramcontent.com/pod-product-compliance
Lightning Source LLC
Chambersburg PA
CBHW070500050426
42449CB00012B/3060